The Tao

Yoga for the Brain

Cristina Smith

Rick Smith

Published by Cristina Smith
Nevada City, CA 95959
www.SudokuWisdom.com

Published through CreateSpace Independent Publishing Platform.

ISBN: 978-1536916355

Stay Sharp! Have Fun! Pencil Me In!

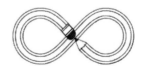

Table of Contents

Introduction

I'm a frequent flyer. After re-reading, yet again, the same in-flight magazine, I realized the dreaded truth. I was bored. I was on my way to visit my brother Rick in Denver. In true desperation, I considered the puzzles. When I saw the Sudoku puzzles I had an almost visceral reaction to them. My inner voice said something like, "Number puzzles- yargh! I don't do those. Seems too much like math."

My skills are in the word and people department, not so much in math and logic. This fateful flight I decided to get over myself and try a Sudoku. I already knew that I wasn't going to be very good at it. I started the easiest one. My suspicion was correct. I was not good at it. In fact, I couldn't figure it out at all.

Rick is a mathematician, professional puzzle and game designer and retired technologist. On the drive to his home from the airport I asked him about Sudoku. I imagined that it was easy and accessible for him. Indeed it was. We enjoyed our visit and after he dropped me off at the airport to head back home, I made a decision. I was going to experiment to see if I could train my mind to shift to a logic mode, and learn to solve the number puzzle of Sudoku.

Thus began my surprising journey of extraordinary evolution through an unassuming 81 square puzzle. It is amazing how sometimes the most unexpected things can trigger the deepest revelations.

Down the Rabbit Hole

I bought a book of 300 easy puzzles at the airport as my self-imposed challenge. I hoped to learn how to shift my perception in that many attempts. I wanted to give myself plenty of allowance for the learning curve and flat out failure. Like learning any new subject, practice and discipline are required to master the technique. Right?

The most amazing thing happened. I delved into the puzzles, and unexpected, deeply spiritual, intuitive information began to come into my consciousness. It arrived in the form of profound sayings. I began to realize that doing Sudoku was not as puzzling as I thought. It was no different than any other activity. How I approached it determined my experience.

With that realization, I began to address the puzzles in a new way. Sudoku, like anything in life, could be approached as a path to further spiritual awakening. As my spiritual teacher, Ingrid Coffin, says in one of her Meta-Thoughts ®

How you do anything is how you do everything.

Spiritual awakening has been, and is, the primary force of movement in my life. This perspective, which applies the spiritual practice of Tao (pronounced 'dao', meaning the path or the way) offers a holistic approach to doing these puzzles. Reasoning, strategy and logic need to be balanced with intuition, noticing and surrender. This concept of wholeness is symbolized by the famous Yin/Yang symbol.

Not only did I need to practice my logical skills, I had to let go of the "I'm no good at math" paradigm. It was essential to surrender my concepts about Sudoku, numbers and my personal abilities. I wanted to allow my intuition to speak, to listen to the whisper within.

I needed to sit with each new puzzle, as though I had never done one before. The goal was to allow logic and intuition to blend alchemically within me. A realization dawned. My work with Sudoku could be approached as part of my path. Ever unfolding enlightenment is the journey, and that journey is my destination.

Enlightenment is a process, not an event.

-Ingrid Coffin

That first book from the airport took me three months to complete. Some were total frustration and others utter bliss. What I learned will last the rest of my life. The best part of the entire process is that Rick and I decided to work together on this book. Logic meets intuition meets logic meets intuition in a continuous loop. Is this a philosophy book or puzzle book? The answer is yes!

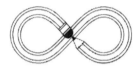

Inside are 100 puzzles ranging from very easy to intermediate and some surprising information on the history and benefits of Sudoku. Each comes with a quote to inspire higher consciousness and meditation. Unattributed quotes are what came to me when doing that first auspicious puzzle book.

May your path to enlightenment be enhanced by the Tao of Sudoku.

Happy puzzling and have fun!

The Tao of Sudoku

What is the Tao? And what does Sudoku have to do with it? A Chinese mystical philosophy founded by Lao-Tzu in the sixth century BCE, the Tao is the symbolic 'path' or 'way' of being. It is seeing all of life's experiences as ongoing practices for the attainment of ever expanding mastery, the road to enlightenment. In this context, it is not a religion but a spiritual and philosophical approach to life.

It is wisdom to know others;

It is enlightenment to know one's self.

The conqueror of men is powerful;

The master of himself is strong.

-Lao-Tzu

Here's the exquisite truth: we are all limitless beings.
Surrender creates room within our consciousness and subtle
bodies (biofield) for more presence and awareness of the
divine nature of each beautiful soul. We can do whatever we
choose. We learn. We grow. We evolve. Doing Sudoku
with intention, mindfulness, and loving kindness towards self
is truly a path to transformation. Even enlightenment!

But don't take my word for it. Find out for yourself with
these 100 puzzles, especially created for this process. Think of
them as 100 steps on the path to self-realization. Each
wisdom saying is as applicable to life as it is to the puzzle.

Everything in your life is there as a vehicle for your transformation. Use it!
-Ram Dass

Let's Play!

Mark up your book!
Make Mistakes!
Respond to the Quotes!
Have Fun!

How to Play

Most Sudoku books have a long section on how to play. Since patience is not my top virtue, I just dove right in and started the first puzzle. I was not willing to look at lots of examples of possible strategies and others' explanations on how I should do this.

These basic guidelines made sense to me:

The goal of Sudoku is to fill all of the 81 squares with the numbers 1-9. Each row across, each column down and each mini 3x3 square within the big 9x9 square will have a 1,2,3,4,5,6,7,8 and 9 in it with no repeats.

The good news is that some of the numbers are already filled in, so there are plenty of clues and hints. Even better, if you get stuck and need a nudge, you can check the answers to get a number to kick start your next move. It's not cheating.

I related it to playing cards. My hand was dealt. I began looking for numbers of a kind and straights/runs from 1-9.

My strategy is to take each number in order and see where they are already filled in. I find it helpful to use the tip of the pencil to tap each number as I see it. This adds the kinesthetic aspect to the mix. Since there can only be one of each number in any row or column, this methodical approach often reveals some answers right away. Doing it in numerical order helps me remember where I am. When I think I have found all nine of kind, I go through the puzzle and tap each one to check my work. I also make sure each number is in the right place. I write the number above the puzzle grid so I know that I don't need to look for it any more.

After the first round of looking for 9 of a kind, then I seek the 1-9 sequences (straights) to see what I can see. I count 1 to 9 in each row, column and mini-square, the pencil tapping the numbers. That helps reduce mistakes due to accidentally misplacing a number. When a row, column or mini-square is complete, I double check with the pencil tap to make sure there are no duplicates or missing numbers. The mind can be tricky!

When you have eliminated the impossible, whatever remains, however improbable, must be the truth.
-Sherlock Holmes (Sir Arthur Conan Doyle)

That sums up how I start a Sudoku. I look for places in the puzzle where I can eliminate all but a single number. For example, in the facing puzzle, the upper right hand mini-square is missing only the numbers 3 and 5.

One of the columns with an empty square already has a 5 in it, so you can also rule out the 5 as a prospect there. The only possible number left is a 3. Elementary, my dear Watson!

Each number that's filled in takes it out of the realm of possible choices from other empty squares in the same row, column and mini-square.

Be willing to shift perspective. Patterns and systems emerge without having to be attached to context and content. Sometimes you can focus on an empty square and see what CAN'T go there. Sometimes focus on a single number (look at the 5s in the facing puzzle and see what comes up). The puzzle will speak to you in your own language. Go with it!

When I finish a Sudoku, on the top I give it a star rating of how well I think I did. This is a final affirmation that I actually succeeded!

1

6				5	8	4	9	7
5	9					8		2
			9	2	6	1		
2	6		7		5			
	5	7				1	2	
		6		9			7	8
	8	9	5	3				
4		6					5	9
1	2	5	9	6				4

The journey of a thousand miles begins with a single step. -Lao-Tzu

2

5				4	8			
	9				1	8	4	7
	6		3	7		2	1	
	3	2				5		4
6	4	8		9		7	3	1
7		1				6	2	
	7	5		3	6		9	
4	2	6	9				7	
			7	2				6

Knowing where to start is sometimes the key to the solution.

3

	8	5		2				
2		6	9	8				
			1		6	2	5	8
	7		4	6			3	9
1	2	3				6	7	4
9	6			1	3		8	
8	3	2	6		4			
				3	8	4		6
				7		8	2	

A good eraser is essential in life.

4

		4		6				8
	1		8		9		4	3
9	3	8				1		
	5	6	3	9	2			1
	8			1			3	
3			7	8	6	2	5	
		5				3	7	4
8	2		9		4		1	
4				7		8		

What isn't shows what is.

9	8		2		1	3	7	
1		2				8		6
	7				6	1	2	
		4	6	2		7		
	2		1		8		6	
		7		9	4	2		
	6	8	3				1	
7		9				6		2
	4	1	7		2		3	8

Slow and steady wins the race. -Aesop

6

2	9	4		8				3
			5	9	2	4		
	1	8			4	7		
8	5			4	1		3	
1	3						7	4
	4		7	3			9	5
		5	6			9	8	
		6	8	1	5			
3				7		2	5	6

Even though the puzzle may look similar, a different approach may be needed.

7

		9	6	2	3	4	7	
	4	8					2	3
		6	7	4			1	
1	9				7			2
6			8	5	4			1
3			1				4	6
	5			7	6			4
4	6					8	5	
	2	3	4	8	5	1		

Keep track of what you have done.

8

		1			7		4	
8	2			4	5	1	7	
		7		1				5
6		4	1			2	9	7
			5	7	6			
7	1	8			9	6		3
1				6		9		
	9	6	3	5			2	8
	7		9			5		

Happiness is catching! Correct your mistakes

with grace.

9

4	9	3				2		
			9		2	8	3	1
	1		7	3	5			
5	4	6		1	3			9
3								4
9			6	2		3	5	8
			3	9	8		1	
1	5	9	2		7			
		7				6	9	2

Knowledge is a treasure, but practice is the key

to it. –Lao-Tzu

10

		8	2	4	1	6	3	
				8		5	7	2
3	9			7				
		3	7		4		1	8
7								3
1	8		6		2	4		
				6			2	5
8	6	5		2				
	3	1	9	5	8	7		

The more you look, the more you see.

Sudoku, Spirituality and Surrender

Sudoku, like anything in life, from making the bed daily, to going on a meditation retreat, to offering healing prayers for a loved one, can be approached as spiritual experience.

It can be a mindfulness practice on the extraordinary journey of personal evolution, often called enlightenment. This common, familiar puzzle may even be approached as a metaphor for the puzzle of ever expanded self-realization through presence, awareness and most of all, surrender. This was my process. First comes surrender.

Surrender to the fact that I do not know how to do this and am not skilled at it. Surrender to the idea that these puzzles are stupid and not worth my time since I have more important things to do. Surrender the outdated opinion of myself that I am not good with numbers or math or puzzles. Surrender my need to succeed immediately.

I had to unstick myself from the concepts of who I thought I was, and what I was able to do or accomplish. I needed to let go of old childhood ideas and paradigms about my abilities. I had to remember to breathe.

Inhale surrender. Exhale surrender.
This surrender was uncomfortable at first.
Later it was a huge relief.

11

				8	2	7		
9			1	7	4	6	5	
		6	9	5		8	1	
4			3					1
	6	1				3	9	
3					5			7
	9	3		2	1	5		
	4	2	5	9	8			3
		5	4	3				

Praise yourself often.

12

	2	1	8	3	9			
9					2	1		5
				6		3		9
1	3	6	2					
	4	2	5		1	9	3	
					3	2	7	1
2		8		5				
3		4	7					2
			3	2	4	8	9	

Mysteries are often revealed slowly.

13

6	8	7	3				1	
			9	7	1	6		8
				6	2		7	
	3	4						9
	5	9	1		3	7	4	
8						5	3	
	6		4	3				
4		1	5	2	8			
	2			6	8	9	4

In oneself lies the whole world, and if you know
how to look and learn, then the door is there
and the key is in your hand. Nobody on earth
can give you either that key or the door to open,
except yourself. –J. Krishnamurti

14

6			7			9		
	1			8				
9		3	1		5	7		4
5					6		3	8
3	4	6		5		1	7	2
2	8		3					5
7		4	5		1	8		3
				7			4	
		5			3			7

Check. Double check.

15

6	3	7	1					
9	5	1		3			4	6
				5		3		
		8	3		1	7	2	
7			2		8			4
	4	2	5		7	6		
		6		2				
3	2			7		5	8	1
					3	4	6	2

**Change your perspective; change the
information.**

16

		2		6			3	9
	7	6	9					
		1	5		4		6	2
5	8		6		7	9		3
				5				
6		7	4		3		8	5
7	1		3		9	2		
					5	3	1	
2	4			7		5		

Create good habits and use them as a
foundation, not a prison.

17

		5			4			3
	3	6	5	7				1
	2	4	3		1			
					2		3	5
8	1	3				9	6	2
5	7		6					
			2		6	1	5	
2				8	5	3	9	
3			7			8		

Perfection is the willingness to be imperfect.

–Lao-Tzu

18

	9					8		7
		3	1	5	8	4		
	5			4				2
5	8	2					7	
7		1	3	8	2	6		5
	6					2	4	8
9				3			2	
		8	2	9	7	5		
6		7					8	

It is good to have faith in yourself.

19

1			8				5	2
6		2				4	8	
8	5				2	3		9
	9	1	6	3		8		
				8				
		8		4	5	1	3	
5		6	1				9	3
	7	3				6		4
9	1				6			8

**The sooner you see your mistakes, the sooner
you can correct them.**

20

7				9		2	8	5
8			7			9		
		2		8	1			
		9	1		8	4		2
2		6		5		7		3
5		1	3		7	8		
			2	7		5		
		8			5			7
4	5	7		1				9

Be patient with yourself.

What Does Math Have to Do with It?

Nothing and everything.

Even though a Sudoku puzzle uses numbers as the symbols within it, those numbers are just convenient characters that are easily recognized. The nine symbols could just as easily be

It does not take any math ability to solve a Sudoku puzzle. Really. If the reaction we feel to seeing a Sudoku puzzle with numbers is "OMG, not a MATH challenge!" we are likely experiencing an outdated sensation based on ancient personal history. That old feeling can be released with an exhale and we can bring ourselves back to the present moment.

The math myth is an immediate brick wall of perception we can dismantle right now. In Sudoku, there is no adding or subtracting. No infinitesimal decimal points or calculus. The numbers do not have a value or meaning. They are basic shapes with which we are all familiar.

According to math people, solving a Sudoku does give that same kind of happy buzz as that of solving a complex equation. At the heart of mathematics, its intuitive essence is about noticing patterns. The logical element is piecing together the why and how of that pattern.

21

2	3			9	4			
		7		6		1		
	1	4	5					3
6		9						
1			6	4	2			9
						6		8
7					6	9	1	
		2		7		4		
			4	2			8	5

Touch ultimate emptiness,

Hold steady and still. -Lao-Tzu

22

		5	7					6
			6			9		7
		7	8					
		8			5	7	9	4
5				2				3
9	3	1	7			5		
					3	6		
8		3		1				
4				5		1		

Follow the rhythm.

23

4	5	2			3			6
		3			5	8		
8			4					
9	4	8		2				
		1		9		6		
				8		5	9	4
					2			1
		4	6			7		
1			7			2	6	5

Course correction takes focus and a shift of perspective.

24

		4	6			1		
	6			2				9
					4	3	5	6
2					6	5		
	5		8	9	3		1	
		8	2					3
1	8	2	7					
6				8			9	
		3			5	2		

Be aware of what is dazzling you. What looks solid at the beginning may fade upon closer inspection.

25

7		8			2			
	1	2				4	9	
	3	6		5	4			
3	7	5						
			3		6			
						8	7	3
			9	6		7	4	
	8	4				9	3	
			4			6		2

When I let go of what I am, I become what I might be. –Lao-Tzu

39

26

		1		6	2			
6			4				1	
4	3				5	6		7
			2			9		8
	7			3			4	
8		5			6			
7		2	3				8	5
	9				7			1
			6	5		7		

Use more than one means to check your work.

27

| 4 | | | | 3 | | | 5 | | 8 |
| 3 | 6 | | | 4 | 2 | | | | | |
					7				6	
		7				4		8		
		6		5	8	3		9		
		2		9				4		
	5			3						
					5	8			4	9
8		1			4					3

Finding a key to one aspect may allow many things to fall into place.

28

	7				5		8	6
6							7	2
				6	1	9		
			1			7	6	9
		6		7		8		
9	4	7			8			
		2	9					
3	6							8
4	8		5		6		3	

Don't be afraid to erase - it is a symbol of strength.

29

					5	4	2	9
1								
	5	2	4	1				
	6		1		4		9	5
2				3				1
5	4		6		9		7	
				5	1	8	6	
6	1	3	8					4

By letting go it all gets done.

–Lao-Tzu

30

5								
3	1		2	4		5		
4			5	8	3	9	1	
	7		4					
		4		9		2		
					6		9	
	5	8	3	1	2			9
		6		7	4		2	5
								7

Different states of being call for different approaches. Be open to who you are in the moment.

The Yoga of Sudoku

Solving the puzzle of Sudoku is a mystical practice, a yoga of the mind. Of the eight limbs of yoga, it fits well in the sixth, *Dharana*, which trains the mind through concentration.

The practice is not about concentrating on something. Its purpose is to help notice distracting mind chatter before the dish runs away with the spoon and return it to the point of focus. Again. And again. And again. And like so many profound spiritual practices, this is simple, but not easy.

As a daily practice, Sudoku can be used to go deeper and learn more about the self. Be patient. It's okay to start by not being good at this. It's okay to make lots of mistakes. That's how we learn.

Accept that there is a learning curve; it gets easier with practice.

To the mind that is still,

the whole universe surrenders.

-Lao-Tzu

31

6		8		7	3		9	
	9							
					6	2	8	7
			5	8	7			2
2								6
5			6	4	2			
8	2	6	1					
							5	
	5		3	6		8		4

Let the mystery reveal itself. It can surprise you.

32

	3	5	6				7	
9	8			1		6		3
	2		3					
				3		4		
		1	4	2	9	7		
		2		5				
					2		8	
2		8		6			5	7
	6				8	2	1	

Notice. What do you notice? Let it emerge.

33

							4	5
		6		1			7	8
3	4	7						2
	2	6	7					
	7		3	1	5		2	
				6	1	9		
4						8	3	9
8	5		4		2			
7	6							

The ancients said, 'Accept and you become whole,'

Once whole, the world is as your home.

–Lao-Tzu

34

3	1		5	7				
		9	6					8
6	5					1	2	
	9				3	4		2
				6				
7		3	4				8	
	2	6					1	4
4					6	2		
				1	4		3	9

When you let go of habitual thinking

new answers arrive.

35

	6				3		1	
2			9	1			6	5
9		1						
	2	9	3			6		
			8	2	4			
		8			9	1	2	
						7		1
5	3			9	6			8
	8		5				9	

My mind is different today.

36

7				1		3		5
2					6	7	8	
		3	9	7				
9	8							
	3		7	4	9		2	
							7	1
				8	5	6		
	7	6	4					3
3		9		2				4

Uncomfortable? Guilty?? Wrong???

Do something you're not good at.

Love yourself anyway.

37

5		2	3					
			9				6	
			2		8	3	9	
7			6				5	1
6			4	5	1			8
1	4			2				6
9	1	4		7				
	7			6				
			9	2			7	

**A good traveler has no fixed plans and is not
intent on arriving.**

–Lao-Tzu

38

2			1			6		
			4	9	6		8	5
	8		3					
6	4	3		2		8		
				4				
		7		1		3	4	2
					4		5	
9	1		7	6	5			
		5			1			8

Sometimes you just call it a learning experience.

39

8	9							
						3	9	1
		2	4	3	9			
		4			7	1	6	
2	7			9			4	3
	1	5	6			7		
			1	2	8			5
4	2	8						
							7	2

Your mind can be tricky in its desire to be right.

40

		2	9				3	
3	9			2			8	
				5	6		9	7
8	4					3		
			2		7			
		7					4	5
2	7		5	8				
	8			3			5	9
	3				9	1		

Are you paying attention?

The Story of Sudoku

The rich historic roots of Sudoku create a tale of mythic proportions. In Chinese literature dating from as early as 2800 BCE, legend says Emperor Yu was walking along the Lo River, and he noticed a turtle with a unique diagram on its shell, a 3x3 square.

In Chinese cosmology, legend placed the world on the back of the turtle. The shell was thought to have markings of heaven and earth.

Turtles ruled the north and represented the element of water. They were considered a symbol of wisdom, endurance, wealth and long life, so the shell pattern definitely had spiritual importance. When delivered to the oracle for shamanic divination, the pattern's cosmic significance was read. It was believed that the 3x3 specific square configuration encapsulated the harmonies of the universe.

The square was called lo shu or "scroll of the river Lo," and eventually became the philosophical basis of the I Ching and Feng Shui.

These techniques analyze the flow of the subtle energies in human situations (I Ching), or the environment (Feng Shui), including homes.

41

	2		1					
						8	3	
		3	4		7	2	5	1
				3		6		9
	8	2				7	4	
1		6		7				
6	5	4	2		8	3		
	7	1						
					6		2	

There is nothing as deceptive as an obvious fact.

-Sir Arthur Conan Doyle

42

6	1	8						
			5	2	8			
	5	9					7	8
1	6	5						
		7	4		9	2		
						1	3	7
7	9					4	2	
			2	3	5			
						8	1	3

One new bit of information can change

everything.

43

		2		1	7		9	3
	4		2	9				
		1				2		
8						5		6
2	1						3	9
6		9						1
		5				9		
				8	4		1	
1	8		5	3		6		

**Sometimes when you look for deeper clues you
miss what's right in front of you.**

44

			6	7			
4	6						
	7	1				6	2
6	4	2					9
3	2	5		4		7	6
7				9		4	1
8	1			3		5	
						9	4
		7	4				

**Learn how much attention you need for
anything.**

45

		6	8	7			9	
2	4		6		5			
	5						4	
					8	5		
6	1	5				3	2	8
		8	3					
	7						3	
			4		9		8	1
	8			3	1	4		

I have just three things to teach: simplicity, patience, compassion. These three are your

greatest treasures. –Lao-Tzu

46

			9	1		7	8	
2			9	1		7		
	9	4	6		5			3
					6	8		
	5	6	8		3	4	1	
		3	7					
1			3		4	2	5	
		9		8	7			1
	4							

Remember to stop when you are behind.

You can always wait until tomorrow.

47

		9	8		1	3	4	
2								
			2			7	9	1
	9		1	3		6	7	
	5	4		7	6		2	
9	4	7		5				
								9
	8	1	3		4	2		

Patience will reveal all.

48

4			1	9				
	9						5	
	5	1	3					6
3		8			7			9
9		4				7		2
1			9			8		4
5					6	1	9	
	3						2	
				5	2			8

Seeking insight is addictive.

49

	8		5					
	2		4		1	9		3
9		1	8	6				
						4	1	5
		9				3		
3	1	8						
				4	9	5		1
6		5	3		7		2	
					5		6	

Life throws up around us these temptations,
these distractions, and the problem is to find
the immovable center within. Then you can
survive anything. -Joseph Campbell

50

	7			3			8	
	3	2			5	6	9	
	6	5		1				
9		3	4					
			6					
				3	9			8
			7			2	4	
	2	1	6			8	3	
	8		5			6		

Notice when you make many mistakes.

Grab your eraser.

Magic Squares

The 3x3 square became known as a magic square. As Sudoku has spread around the world in current times, so magic squares traveled the world over the centuries, and were used as a powerful tool.

Priests, sages, and healers in Tibet, Japan, Thailand, Egypt, Arabia, Europe and Africa, throughout the centuries believed that magic squares were small models of the Universe. Christians, Muslims, Jews and Hindus have all used magic squares in some form or fashion. Magic squares embodied the theory of 'As above, So below.' This philosophy was first published in Arabic, in the Emerald Tablet, 500-700 CE. The belief was that if the correct number formula was displayed, people could be influenced. Magic!!

Sudoku is an evolution of the magic square, called the Latin square, which was developed by Swiss mathematician Leonhard Euler in the 1700s. Also in the 18ᵗʰ century, Benjamin Franklin used the magic square to solve mathematical problems. From then until the 20ᵗʰ century, the magic square was mostly considered an esoteric mathematics conundrum.

In 1979, the first publication of modern Sudoku appeared in the magazine Dell Pencil Puzzles and Word Games by Howard Garns and was called *Number Place*. It gained popularity in Japan during the 1980s, and was picked up in 2004 by the British newspaper, The Times. The word sudoku means single number in Japanese.

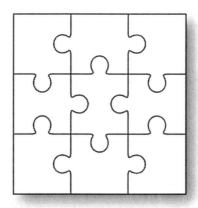

Now virtually every periodical has a Sudoku puzzle. There was even one in very small print on the instructions included with the printer ink cartridge! It has become ubiquitous. Magically!

What makes a magic square magic? It is the *magic constant* which means that the sum of every row, column and diagonal is the same. In modern Sudoku, the magic constant is 45, which is the sum of 1+2+3+4+5+6+7+8+9. In numerology, numbers are often reduced to a single digit to provide divinatory meaning. So for Sudoku, the number to consider is 4+5, which equals 9.

In this way of thinking, every time a Sudoku puzzle is completed, a magic square is created. It has the properties of the number 9. In numerology, 9 is often associated with completion.

The completion of a Sudoku puzzle, a magic square of 9, can be viewed from a philosophical perspective. It is making the will visible, success insured, completion possible, insight gathered, and another step forward on the road to enlightenment taken.

51

	6						9	
9				6	1	2		
		5	9			8	3	
2		8		7				
	1		2	8	3		7	
				1		3		8
	8	7			6	4		
		4	1	2				3
	2						8	

The first dazzle takes time to truly reveal its depths.

		6		1	7	4		
		1	4					2
9			8					7
					2	7	5	
	9		3		6		1	
	1	3	7					
1					9			5
4					1	3		
		5	2	4		9		

The better you know your subject, the more you know what to look for and the deeper you see.

53

			5			2		4
	4			8	6			
5				3	4	7		8
					3	5		
	9						7	
		6	7					
8		4	3	7				6
			6	4			1	
9		5			2			

Nature does not hurry, yet everything is

accomplished.

–Lao-Tzu

54

9	7			2				
8	4	2			9			
				4	6			2
								6
6	2		3	9	8		4	7
3								
1		8	2					
			5			7	1	3
				3			8	4

The moment you think you have it all figured

out is the moment you get sloppy.

						8	2	
1				8			5	4
	2	8						9
		1	9	2				6
4				3				5
8				1	4	9		
2						3	7	
3	7			5				2
	1	6						

You can't see everything at once.

Some things need a second look.

56

6				2				
							9	
				6	1	4	7	2
1		6	3			8		
5	4			1			3	7
		7			6	1		5
7	8	1	6	4				
	9							
				5				1

Sometimes the first thing you see is an illusion.

57

					3	9	4	5
	7				1		2	
		2	8	5			6	
4		7	5					
6								8
					6	4		2
	9			7	5	3		
	6		1				9	
7	3	8	9					

The You are bright, it is said,

If you see what is small;

A store of small strengths

Makes you strong. -Lao-Tzu

58

7				8	5	3		6
	2		6		7		1	
			4	2				
						5		4
8				5				9
1		6						
				6	8			
	6		2		9		5	
4		2	5	7				3

Persistence and patience lead to ease and flow.

59

		2	3		4	5		
6								
				1	5	2	7	
						4	8	5
		4	7		6	9		
2	9	5						
	4	3	5	7				
								9
		9	4		2	7		

Numbers can be flexible.

60

5			3	9		8		
		6			2	3		
	8			7		9		
					1	2		
1	4						3	7
		5	4					
		7		2			8	
		3	9			7		
		1		5	4			3

Sometimes I am not as smart as I think I am.

Step into the Mystery

A Sudoku is solving a mystery with the clues available. It has 81 squares and there is only one correct answer. There are enough numbers given from the start to get to the solution. And, just like solving mystery stories, self-expression through a favorite art form, cooking, or any other repeated activity, one develops certain ways and strategies of how to approach each different (yet similar) situation. That's why people can get so excited about Sudoku and end up doing many of them. It is the enchantment of the mystery, and the high of the solution that keeps folks coming back for more.

There's another layer of appeal when in the Tao of Sudoku. Each single puzzle can allow a move into mindfulness, a meditative state of being. It can enhance awareness and teach inner insight into self.

That said, the mathematics of Sudoku is at the heart of some very powerful codes that make this whole information and communication age possible. From a text message, to a picture or a cell phone conversation, math is used to convert the message into a string of numbers so it can be electronically transmitted and received.

As the message is sent across wires or bounced between satellites, things can go wrong. Error can be introduced by noise in the system, possibly caused by faulty equipment, weak signals, atmosphere or any number of other factors. We have all experienced the result of these code errors. That's when the call is dropped, or the picture attached to the text doesn't go through, or the email won't send.

Think of a completed Sudoku as a packet of information with only one correct configuration, like a photo. This message originally had 81 characters, but many of them have been lost due to a glitch in the matrix.

The internal logic of the Sudoku means that it's possible to recover the complete message from the remaining numbers.

The mathematics used to encode digital messages works similarly. The logic within the message allows information to be recovered even when some of it is lost during transmission. This error correction magic square technology is a key in picture transmissions from space. This began as far back as 1972, when the Mariner space probe flew past Mars. It is still important in the space program.

In 2006, Toshiba patented its "magic square algorithm," which allows an 18-bit LCD panel to produce picture quality equivalent to a 24-bit LCD panel, with up to 16 million colors.

We also use magic square math in statistical analysis, agriculture, and three, four, multi-dimensional and even infinite geometry. Fractals, sacred geometry, art and music are also related to the magic square.

Coming full circle, notice that math really does have nothing and everything to do with Sudoku. Like all great metaphysical paradoxes, it is beyond duality and may be approached as a path to the Great Mystery, the Tao.

61

		3	6		7		1	
		6		3				4
	2							3
	6	4	7		8			
		9				7		
			4		5	9	6	
5							9	
4				7		8		
	8		2		9	4		

When you accept yourself, the whole world

accepts you. –Lao-Tzu

62

					3		9	
8	6		1	7			2	
	2	9						
7	9		3					4
5				8				9
2					4		6	1
						6	1	
	5			6	2		4	8
	3		8					

**Look again. Your first impression is only the
beginning.**

63

4				7				
				8	9	9	2	1
3				9	6	7		
	7		1					
		6	4	9	3	1		
				7		5		
	1	8	7					5
7	6	4	5					
			8				6

Inhale. Exhale. All is well.

64

3	1	7	9	8	4			
							7	
			5		3			
1	8					5		3
			8		2			
9		4					8	6
			1		8			
	6							
			6	3	7	4	1	9

Sometimes you just need to see the right

context to get the right answer.

65

					5			4
	2						3	9
3			2					6
	5			7		9	6	
	6			5			2	
	9	7		8			4	
5					8			3
9	1						7	
2			1					

The Way can be neither sensed nor known:
It transmits sensation and transcends
knowledge. -Lao-Tzu

Puzzle Pointers from Cristina: Progress and Play

At first glance, I saw in Sudoku a challenge to accept and master. After completing hundreds of them, it was surprising to recognize that this supposedly straightforward puzzle had its own magic. My logical abilities became more finely honed the more I sharpened my pencil and played. And erased. It was similar to the remarkable results and rewards of the countless hours I spent honing my intuitive skills. With Sudoku, it was as though a veil of logic fogginess was lifted and some of its beautiful mystery was revealed in a series of "aha!" moments.

Learning Sudoku is a skill, like learning a new language. First the words are learned separately and then tentatively put together. Initially, you have to translate what you want to say in your head, say it, then hear the response, translate that to English, determine your response in English then translate that in your head to the other language, then speak it. After a while, the interim translation steps disappear and the words begin to flow.

As my skills grew, a new element of cognitive vision started to happen when I first looked at a Sudoku. Now, a kind of bird's eye overview, like a *puzzle vision super power* happens and I notice the numbers as shapes. The traditional mathematical values have become meaningless. The sensuous curves of the 3s, the triumphant triangles of the 4s, and the elegant intertwining of the 8s are what I see. I notice where shapes are missing. I enjoy the eye flow of the number shapes game. This is actually fun! My brain really has become more flexible and playful!

When I finish my initial scan, then I begin my poker hand system. The more confident I become, the more important it is to have a good eraser.

Doveryai, no proveryai.
(Trust, but verify.) –
Russian proverb made famous by Ronald Reagan

I notice that my spatial awareness has improved. In the Sudoku puzzle, if I fill in a number, say a 7, in one mini-square, I can use my *puzzle vision* to scan all of the other squares simultaneously.

Sometimes with that glance, I see where the remaining missing 7's go in each of the mini-squares so I can get nine of a kind. I can see in many directions at the same time, which seems weird but is cool to experience.

It is a bit much to think that a seemingly senseless and silly practice like learning how to do Sudoku puzzles can provide such profound results. Yet it did. It showed me that I had previously limited myself. I am as capable as I choose to be, even with number puzzles. It's all about whether I choose to apply myself.

66

		6	8		9	7	4	
		1			6			
							6	
		7			3			8
9	1	4		6		3	7	2
3			7			9		
	5							
			3			8		
	7	3	4		5	1		

Develop a strategy and then be open to flow.

67

		9	4	6	1			
		7		3		1	9	6
1		8			4		2	
	7		2			9		5
3	9	1		2		7		
			5	7	3	6		

A need for result can make your eyes fool you.

68

			4	5	6		1	8
			4	5	6		1	3
	3				1		6	7
1				4	5		7	
7								6
	6		1	3				5
3	9		7				8	
5	1		9	8	2			
4								

Listen. Hear what speaks to you.

69

			7	5			9	8
		3	2				1	
	7	5				3		
					2			
7	6		1		5		8	3
			6					
		4				1	5	
	1				7	6		
6	3			4	1			

Take care with the end as you do with the beginning. –Lao-Tzu

70

		9	7		3	2		
7	6			2				
			9			1		
							7	2
2	9		6	1	7		5	4
5	4							
		6			4			
				6			8	1
		3	1		9	5		

When you feel like you've lost your touch,
go back to the basics.

Stay Sharp with Sudoku!

Disease Prevention, Delay and Intervention

A number of recent research studies on brain health, disease prevention, neuropsychology and gerontology have used Sudoku as a means of experimental intervention. The results have been resoundingly positive and encouraging.* In the scientific medical community, emerging literature suggests that lifestyle factors may play an important role in reducing age-related cognitive decline.

"*Cognitively stimulating leisure activities*" is the medical/scientific term that includes puzzles. One study that included 65,000 participants suggested that frequently engaging in Sudoku or similar puzzles was significantly helpful with grammatical reasoning, spatial working memory and episodic memory scores. The benefits of puzzles were even found to continue to positively impact cognitive functioning and brain health when measured and analyzed two years later.

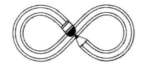

* Published on the US Department of Health & Human Services, National Institutes of Health, National Center for Biotechnology Information website.

Sudoku training may even help improve the cognitive strategies used by Parkinson's disease patients in problem solving. Practice with the puzzle has been shown to assist people and their brains in improving the ability to generate internally applicable rules. Besides, it's fun!

Imagine! Sudoku may soon be considered a non-psychopharmacological intervention to assist in enhanced whole brain functioning.

71

				6	9		7	1
9	7	4			2			
	3							
	1						2	3
		8		1		7		
6	4						1	
							6	
			7			5	3	9
3	8		2	5				

Sometimes you need to look for what can't be there to see what can be.

72

1	7		6					
						5		2
6	2	9		8	5	1		
				7				6
	5			6			1	
7				4				
		7	2	9		8	4	5
9		8						
					1		7	9

New clues are revealed as you look deeper.

73

7	3		2					
					6		8	5
			4					
3		8					5	1
		2	1	7	5	4		
1	5					2		9
					3			
5	6		9					
					2		4	3

The follower of knowledge learns
as much as he can every day;
The follower of the Way forgets
as much as he can every day. –Lao-Tzu

74

1							5	
4	7		2					
							6	4
3		1		7	4			
		5		2		8		
			1	9		6		3
8	4							
					9		3	5
	3							9

Full presence induces awareness.

Oversights and mistakes fall away.

75

3							7	
				7		4		
5	4		2	6		9		
	3			4		7	2	8
4	1	2		3			6	
		9		8	7		3	6
		3		5				
	2							7

Seeing is a result of looking with other eyes.

76

			5	3				4
		4			2			8
							7	9
	3			5		1		
	6	1	3		4	7	9	
		9		6			5	
4	7							
9			8			2		
6				9	3			

Persistence and patience lead to ease and flow.

77

		2	3					
7			2		6		8	
		9			4	2		
4				7		8	3	5
1	2	8		3				6
		1	8			5		
	8		4		9			1
					1	9		

Let it be still, and it will gradually become clear.

–Lao-Tzu

78

	1							
3	6			1	7			8
7				3	9		5	
		7						6
8		2		4		3		9
1						8		
	7		6	9				3
5			3	7			6	4
							7	

Patterns are revealed through focused

perseverance.

79

	2							
1	3		9		7			
		6			4	3	1	8
6	9	1	5					
					9	4	8	6
8	1	3	7			6		
			8		3		9	2
						3		

It's okay to ask for help.

80

2											
			1				4	
8			2	4		7	3	
	4	6	8			5		
		8	3	5	9	1		
		1			6	8	9	
	6	2		8	3			9
	8				4			
								5

Get to know yourself in different states of mind.

Allow new perspectives to emerge.

Our Ever Evolving Brains
Better Living Through Neuroplasticity

The discovery of neuroplasticity is as important to brain science as the realization that the Earth is not flat.

Conventional wisdom was that the brain stopped developing after the first few years of life. This was the only time the brain's neurons were able to form connections and was considered 'plastic.' That led scientists to believe that if a particular area of the adult brain was damaged, the nerve cells could not form new connections or regenerate, and the functions controlled by that area of the brain would be permanently lost.

Fortunately, current scientific research recognizes that the brain is superbly supple and continues to reorganize itself by forming new neural connections throughout life. This phenomenon, called *neuroplasticity*, provides us with an ever evolving brain.

It effectively adapts to changes caused by damage, as well as exquisitely adjusts to any and all experiences and transformations we may encounter. This frees us from merely reacting to situations and stimuli due to genetically determined hardwiring or long ingrained habit. We each have the ability and opportunity to train and re-program our brains at will.

Approaching life with the attitude of a lifetime learner, we can achieve better living through neuroplasticity to enrich our personal evolution. Training in any new skill requires consistent, enthusiastic effort over time.

Practice, failure, patience, and openness are essential on the path. It is the Tao.

9	5	6			2			
1						2		9
2		4	3			8		
				3	8			
		9				6		
			4	5				
		8			9	7		3
6		2						8
			8			5	4	6

There is nothing you can do that's more important than being fulfilled.

-Joseph Campbell

82

		7			5			8
9	3	6			2	5		
		7				9		
8	1	9					3	
	7					6	9	5
		1		8				
		8	1			3	4	6
5			4			1		

There is a difference between looking and seeing.

83

		8	5					
	4		7		9	5	6	
3						9		
	6	2						
7	9						4	6
						3	2	
		5						9
	8	7	9		1		5	
					4	2		

The place where something can't go may reveal

where it belongs.

84

6	3		2					
	9	8						
		7		9	4		8	
				2	9	4		
		2	7		6	1		
		4	3	1				
	7		6	5		8		
						2	1	
					1		9	7

Experience reveals new strategies.

85

7	3	9						
			1					
	1		9		4	7		
	7		5		9			4
8								2
4			3		8		9	
		2	6		7		8	
					2			
						4	2	3

The further one goes, the less one knows.

–Lao-Tzu

86

			3			7		6
		8			9		3	
3	6						1	
				5		3		2
7								1
1		9		4				
	1						5	3
	5		7			4		
9		6			2			

Many roads lead to the key.

Be flexible on the path.

87

		2	4			9		
			6	5				
			9		1	8		3
1	5							4
		7				1		
9							3	7
4		8	3		6			
				7	2			
		9			4	7		

Overconfidence can breed carelessness.

88

			8					
1		5	6	9				
9		2				6	5	
4		9	5					
	7						1	
					2	4		6
	4	8				2		9
				2	6	5		4
				4				

Logic is the beginning of wisdom, not the end.

-Mr. Spock

89

		2	5			4	8	1
			8		7		2	6
		3	7	6		8		
9								3
		7		3	4	6		
1	2		9		6			
4	8	9			1	5		

The more blanks you fill in, the easier it is to see the big picture.

90

6		2			3			7
3				5				
		4	9		2		8	
		1						
	3	7		9		4	6	
						7		
	2		6		7	5		
				1				6
4			8			9		2

Once you know what you are looking for,

it is easier to find it.

Brains Just Want to Have Fun

Sudoku is an engaging way to train the brain by accessing its inherent neuroplasticity. The puzzle appeals to both our creative and logical minds, our right and left brain hemispheres.

If one approaches life predominantly from a right brain perspective, Sudoku is an easy and effective way to strengthen left brain skills. If left brain oriented, the yoga of Sudoku is an accessible and successful way to enhance and encourage right brain abilities.

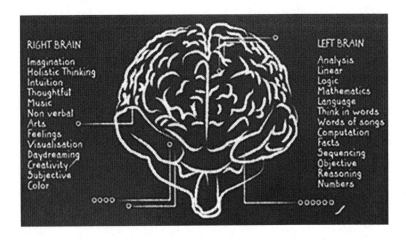

This synergy between the left and right brain can result in improved memory, deeper learning, increased recall, better hand-eye coordination and boosted self-esteem. Isn't it amazing how playing a game can improve cognitive health and encourage a whole brain approach to life?

How does Sudoku work to help the brain? First, it is fun. Most of us would rather play an entertaining game than do something that seems like work. Next it is a strategy game, not a game of chance, like one using dice. The key to how the game unfolds is individual. We each solve things differently; it is a journey of self-discovery.

Sudoku is complex enough to keep us mentally engaged. It is simple enough so we don't get lost in a maze of rules. It teaches shifting perspectives and how to stay aware and alert. By noticing similarities and differences, we enhance cognition of patterns, and generally help the brain be flexible and adaptable.

Sudoku is of a limited duration, 81 squares, and can be repeated in numerous iterations. In the fun fact department, the number of unique Sudoku puzzles possible (as calculated in 2005 by Ed Russell and Frazer Jarvis) is 5,472,730,538.

Best of all, we get the reward of a super shot of brain bliss when each Sudoku is successfully solved. Yes! Dopamine, the neurotransmitter that helps control the brain's reward and pleasure centers, is released into the brain and gives us that "I did it!" lift when we accomplish what we set out to do. It makes us want to come back for more pleasure through positive puzzling.

91

9	2				7			
				6			2	9
		6					7	
	9	8			1	3		7
				3				
3		4	6			1	9	
	3					5		
5	8			9				
			5				3	8

Approach each new puzzle with curiosity and wonder.

92

7			4					3
	8	2	9					5
			5				2	
				9	1		4	
		8				5		
	3		7	6				
	7			1				
1					9	6	8	
2					4			7

There isn't anything except your own life that can be used as ground for your spiritual practice. Spiritual practice is your life, twenty-four hours a day. -Pema Chödrön

93

	9		3	8				
3	1	6	4					
		2			9			
	6					1		7
		4		7		6		
2		8						3
			6			3		
					4	5	7	6
				1	7		2	

Keep your brain flexible.

Your insight will see things your mind cannot.

94

6	9							
3			7					
	2				4	8	6	7
4			1	5	7			
			2	4	9			3
9	4	2	6				3	
					2			9
							5	1

What can I learn about myself today?

95

							4	
			7	2			5	8
						1	7	
		2	8		3	9	1	
	8		1		7		6	
	9	1	6		5	8		
	2	6						
5	7		4	1				
	1							

Expect success and be open to how it comes.

Delight in the result.

96

		4				6		
			7		6		5	2
	2			8		3	1	
1				6				
2			8		3			9
				1				6
	3	7		5			8	
8	5		4		1			
		1				5		

By letting go, it all gets done;

The world is won by those who let it go!

But when you try and try,

The world is then beyond the winning.

–Lao-Tzu

97

6		2			9	4		
3	5							
	8	9	2					
		7			1			5
	1	3		8		2	4	
2			5			9		
					2	1	8	
							2	3
		1	3			5		9

One key can open many interdependent locks.

98

3	5				7		1	
7		9		8			5	6
		6	1	5	4	7		
		4	9	3	6	1		
6	4			1		5		2
	3		8				4	9

The only person you can change is yourself.

99

	6							
2	7	1			4			8
5	9		2	3				6
6					9		5	
				7				
	1		8					9
1				4	6		2	5
9			3			6	4	1
							7	

Every step is on the path.

–Lao-Tzu

100

						5	8	6
			5	9	4	1		7
		5		6		2	7	
	4			1			5	
	7	3		4		9		
4		1	7	3	9			
6	3	9						

It had long since come to my attention that people of accomplishment rarely sat back and let things happen to them. They went out and happened to things. -Leonardo da Vinci

Woo Hoo!
You Did It!
Congratulations!

Great Work!

Endgame

Thousands of puzzles after that fascinating trip to Denver, I proudly carry a large pink eraser with me everywhere along with a pencil and Sudoku book. Now, it is fun to erase! I don't have nagging guilty feelings creeping up about making mistakes, making my face flush. In fact I am more aware of my errors and tend to rush less. Patience may be moving up on the list of my virtues!

Sudokus and people have a lot in common. Both are made up of cells, 81 in a Sudoku and 37.2 trillion in a human. Those cells are uniquely arranged in an individual puzzle and person, making each an inimitable expression of extraordinary possibility. They are coherent unto themselves and when there are pieces missing, both may seek solutions for filling in the missing elements to create wholeness.

The level of difficulty varies and what may look crystal clear at first glance could unfold a mystery of mythic proportions. Many false starts, course corrections and erased errors offer learning experiences. Perseverance, awareness and self-acceptance further the journey. When that process is complete, a puzzle is solved. A healing or making whole has occurred. After taking time to enjoy the feelings of accomplishment, it's on to the next challenge.

Through the physiological miracle of neuroplasticity, the brain can be re-wired through practicing the yoga of Sudoku.

After all, Sudoku has a long lineage of healing in its evolution from the ancient magic square.

By choosing the Tao of Sudoku as a vehicle on your path of enlightenment, the alchemy has uniquely occurred within. The blending of reasoning, strategy and logic with intuition, noticing and surrender has created change. How does it feel? Is your brain more flexible? Do you notice any changes in your inner landscape?

Last time I talked to Rick, I asked him which level of super hard Sudoku book he is playing. Imagine my delight when he said the same level I was now doing! Yes! From "I'm no good at math puzzles," to healthy sibling rivalry with my ever brilliant brother, I have arrived! Makes me feel pretty good about this process and its results. Best of all, these puzzles are now big fun for me! Love that dopamine bliss buzz!

Wishing you wisdom, wealth, insight, deepening consciousness and an ever playful brain! And fun!

Remember fun!

Answers

At the center of your being

You have the answer;

You know who you are

And you know what you want.

-Lao-Tzu

1

6	1	2	3	5	8	4	9	7
5	9	4	1	7	6	8	3	2
8	7	3	4	9	2	6	1	5
2	6	8	7	1	5	9	4	3
9	5	7	8	4	3	1	2	6
3	4	1	6	2	9	5	7	8
7	8	9	5	3	4	2	6	1
4	3	6	2	8	1	7	5	9
1	2	5	9	6	7	3	8	4

2

5	1	7	2	4	8	9	6	3
2	9	3	6	5	1	8	4	7
8	6	4	3	7	9	2	1	5
9	3	2	1	6	7	5	8	4
6	4	8	5	9	2	7	3	1
7	5	1	4	8	3	6	2	9
1	7	5	8	3	6	4	9	2
4	2	6	9	1	5	3	7	8
3	8	9	7	2	4	1	5	6

3

4	8	5	3	2	7	9	6	1
2	1	6	9	8	5	3	4	7
3	9	7	1	4	6	2	5	8
5	7	8	4	6	2	1	3	9
1	2	3	8	5	9	6	7	4
9	6	4	7	1	3	5	8	2
8	3	2	6	9	4	7	1	5
7	5	1	2	3	8	4	9	6
6	4	9	5	7	1	8	2	3

4

5	7	4	1	6	3	9	2	8
6	1	2	8	5	9	7	4	3
9	3	8	2	4	7	1	6	5
7	5	6	3	9	2	4	8	1
2	8	9	4	1	5	6	3	7
3	4	1	7	8	6	2	5	9
1	9	5	6	2	8	3	7	4
8	2	7	9	3	4	5	1	6
4	6	3	5	7	1	8	9	2

5

 6

9	8	6	2	5	1	3	7	4
1	5	2	4	3	7	8	9	6
4	7	3	9	8	6	1	2	5
8	9	4	6	2	3	7	5	1
3	2	5	1	7	8	4	6	9
6	1	7	5	9	4	2	8	3
2	6	8	3	4	9	5	1	7
7	3	9	8	1	5	6	4	2
5	4	1	7	6	2	9	3	8

2	9	4	1	8	7	5	6	3
7	6	3	5	9	2	4	1	8
5	1	8	3	6	4	7	2	9
8	5	7	9	4	1	6	3	2
1	3	9	2	5	6	8	7	4
6	4	2	7	3	8	1	9	5
4	7	5	6	2	3	9	8	1
9	2	6	8	1	5	3	4	7
3	8	1	4	7	9	2	5	6

 7

 8

5	1	9	6	2	3	4	7	8
7	4	8	5	1	9	6	2	3
2	3	6	7	4	8	9	1	5
1	9	4	3	6	7	5	8	2
6	7	2	8	5	4	3	9	1
3	8	5	1	9	2	7	4	6
8	5	1	9	7	6	2	3	4
4	6	7	2	3	1	8	5	9
9	2	3	4	8	5	1	6	7

5	6	1	8	9	7	3	4	2
8	2	3	6	4	5	1	7	9
9	4	7	2	1	3	8	6	5
6	5	4	1	3	8	2	9	7
2	3	9	5	7	6	4	8	1
7	1	8	4	2	9	6	5	3
1	8	5	7	6	2	9	3	4
4	9	6	3	5	1	7	2	8
3	7	2	9	8	4	5	1	6

9

4	9	3	1	8	6	2	7	5
7	6	5	9	4	2	8	3	1
2	1	8	7	3	5	9	4	6
5	4	6	8	1	3	7	2	9
3	8	2	5	7	9	1	6	4
9	7	1	6	2	4	3	5	8
6	2	4	3	9	8	5	1	7
1	5	9	2	6	7	4	8	3
8	3	7	4	5	1	6	9	2

10

5	7	8	2	4	1	6	3	9
4	1	6	3	8	9	5	7	2
3	9	2	5	7	6	1	8	4
6	5	3	7	9	4	2	1	8
7	2	4	8	1	5	9	6	3
1	8	9	6	3	2	4	5	7
9	4	7	1	6	3	8	2	5
8	6	5	4	2	7	3	9	1
2	3	1	9	5	8	7	4	6

11

5	1	4	6	8	2	7	3	9
9	3	8	1	7	4	6	5	2
7	2	6	9	5	3	8	1	4
4	5	7	3	6	9	2	8	1
2	6	1	8	4	7	3	9	5
3	8	9	2	1	5	4	6	7
8	9	3	7	2	1	5	4	6
6	4	2	5	9	8	1	7	3
1	7	5	4	3	6	9	2	8

12

5	2	1	8	3	9	7	6	4
9	6	3	4	7	2	1	8	5
4	8	7	1	6	5	3	2	9
1	3	6	2	9	7	5	4	8
7	4	2	5	8	1	9	3	6
8	5	9	6	4	3	2	7	1
2	7	8	9	5	6	4	1	3
3	9	4	7	1	8	6	5	2
6	1	5	3	2	4	8	9	7

13

6	8	7	3	4	5	9	1	2
3	4	2	9	7	1	6	5	8
9	1	5	8	6	2	4	7	3
1	3	4	6	5	7	2	8	9
2	5	9	1	8	3	7	4	6
8	7	6	2	9	4	5	3	1
7	6	8	4	3	9	1	2	5
4	9	1	5	2	8	3	6	7
5	2	3	7	1	6	8	9	4

14

6	5	8	7	3	4	9	2	1
4	1	7	9	8	2	3	5	6
9	2	3	1	6	5	7	8	4
5	7	9	2	1	6	4	3	8
3	4	6	8	5	9	1	7	2
2	8	1	3	4	7	6	9	5
7	9	4	5	2	1	8	6	3
1	3	2	6	7	8	5	4	9
8	6	5	4	9	3	2	1	7

15

6	3	7	1	8	4	2	9	5
9	5	1	7	3	2	8	4	6
2	8	4	6	5	9	3	1	7
5	6	8	3	4	1	7	2	9
7	9	3	2	6	8	1	5	4
1	4	2	5	9	7	6	3	8
4	1	6	8	2	5	9	7	3
3	2	9	4	7	6	5	8	1
8	7	5	9	1	3	4	6	2

16

4	5	2	7	6	1	8	3	9
3	7	6	9	2	8	4	5	1
8	9	1	5	3	4	7	6	2
5	8	4	6	1	7	9	2	3
1	3	9	8	5	2	6	7	4
6	2	7	4	9	3	1	8	5
7	1	5	3	8	9	2	4	6
9	6	8	2	4	5	3	1	7
2	4	3	1	7	6	5	9	8

17

1	8	5	9	2	4	6	7	3
9	3	6	5	7	8	2	4	1
7	2	4	3	6	1	5	8	9
6	4	9	8	1	2	7	3	5
8	1	3	4	5	7	9	6	2
5	7	2	6	9	3	4	1	8
4	9	8	2	3	6	1	5	7
2	6	7	1	8	5	3	9	4
3	5	1	7	4	9	8	2	6

18

1	9	4	6	2	3	8	5	7
2	7	3	1	5	8	4	6	9
8	5	6	7	4	9	1	3	2
5	8	2	9	6	4	3	7	1
7	4	1	3	8	2	6	9	5
3	6	9	5	7	1	2	4	8
9	1	5	8	3	6	7	2	4
4	3	8	2	9	7	5	1	6
6	2	7	4	1	5	9	8	3

19

1	4	9	8	6	3	7	5	2
6	3	2	7	5	9	4	8	1
8	5	7	4	1	2	3	6	9
4	9	1	6	3	7	8	2	5
3	6	5	2	8	1	9	4	7
7	2	8	9	4	5	1	3	6
5	8	6	1	7	4	2	9	3
2	7	3	5	9	8	6	1	4
9	1	4	3	2	6	5	7	8

20

7	1	4	6	9	3	2	8	5
8	6	5	7	4	2	9	3	1
9	3	2	5	8	1	6	7	4
3	7	9	1	6	8	4	5	2
2	8	6	4	5	9	7	1	3
5	4	1	3	2	7	8	9	6
1	9	3	2	7	4	5	6	8
6	2	8	9	3	5	1	4	7
4	5	7	8	1	6	3	2	9

21

2	3	6	1	9	4	8	5	7
8	5	7	2	6	3	1	9	4
9	1	4	5	8	7	2	6	3
6	2	9	7	3	8	5	4	1
1	8	5	6	4	2	3	7	9
4	7	3	9	1	5	6	2	8
7	4	8	3	5	6	9	1	2
5	9	2	8	7	1	4	3	6
3	6	1	4	2	9	7	8	5

22

1	9	5	3	7	4	2	8	6
3	8	2	5	6	1	9	4	7
6	4	7	8	9	2	3	5	1
2	6	8	1	3	5	7	9	4
5	7	4	6	2	9	8	1	3
9	3	1	7	4	8	5	6	2
7	1	9	4	8	3	6	2	5
8	5	3	2	1	6	4	7	9
4	2	6	9	5	7	1	3	8

23

4	5	2	8	7	3	9	1	6
6	9	3	2	1	5	8	4	7
8	1	7	4	6	9	3	5	2
9	4	8	5	2	6	1	7	3
5	7	1	3	9	4	6	2	8
3	2	6	1	8	7	5	9	4
7	6	5	9	3	2	4	8	1
2	8	4	6	5	1	7	3	9
1	3	9	7	4	8	2	6	5

24

5	9	4	6	3	8	1	2	7
3	6	7	5	2	1	8	4	9
8	2	1	9	7	4	3	5	6
2	3	9	4	1	6	5	7	8
7	5	6	8	9	3	4	1	2
4	1	8	2	5	7	9	6	3
1	8	2	7	4	9	6	3	5
6	4	5	3	8	2	7	9	1
9	7	3	1	6	5	2	8	4

25

7	4	8	1	9	2	3	5	6
5	1	2	6	8	3	4	9	7
9	3	6	7	5	4	1	2	8
3	7	5	8	4	1	2	6	9
8	2	9	3	7	6	5	1	4
4	6	1	5	2	9	8	7	3
2	5	3	9	6	8	7	4	1
6	8	4	2	1	7	9	3	5
1	9	7	4	3	5	6	8	2

26

9	5	1	7	6	2	8	3	4
6	2	7	4	8	3	5	1	9
4	3	8	1	9	5	6	2	7
3	4	6	2	7	1	9	5	8
2	7	9	5	3	8	1	4	6
8	1	5	9	4	6	2	7	3
7	6	2	3	1	9	4	8	5
5	9	4	8	2	7	3	6	1
1	8	3	6	5	4	7	9	2

27

4	7	9	1	3	6	5	2	8
3	6	8	4	2	5	7	9	1
2	1	5	8	9	7	3	6	4
9	3	7	2	6	4	8	1	5
1	4	6	5	8	3	9	7	2
5	8	2	9	7	1	4	3	6
6	5	4	3	1	9	2	8	7
7	2	3	6	5	8	1	4	9
8	9	1	7	4	2	6	5	3

28

1	7	3	2	9	5	4	8	6
6	9	5	8	3	4	1	7	2
8	2	4	7	6	1	9	5	3
5	3	8	1	4	2	7	6	9
2	1	6	3	7	9	8	4	5
9	4	7	6	5	8	3	2	1
7	5	2	9	8	3	6	1	4
3	6	1	4	2	7	5	9	8
4	8	9	5	1	6	2	3	7

29

4	7	6	2	9	8	5	1	3
1	3	8	7	6	5	4	2	9
9	5	2	4	1	3	7	8	6
3	6	7	1	8	4	2	9	5
2	8	9	5	3	7	6	4	1
5	4	1	6	2	9	3	7	8
7	9	4	3	5	1	8	6	2
6	1	3	8	7	2	9	5	4
8	2	5	9	4	6	1	3	7

30

5	8	2	9	6	1	4	7	3
3	1	9	2	4	7	5	6	8
4	6	7	5	8	3	9	1	2
9	7	1	4	2	5	8	3	6
6	3	4	7	9	8	2	5	1
8	2	5	1	3	6	7	9	4
7	5	8	3	1	2	6	4	9
1	9	6	8	7	4	3	2	5
2	4	3	6	5	9	1	8	7

31

6	4	8	2	7	3	1	9	5
7	9	2	8	1	5	4	6	3
3	1	5	4	9	6	2	8	7
9	6	1	5	8	7	3	4	2
2	8	4	9	3	1	5	7	6
5	7	3	6	4	2	9	1	8
8	2	6	1	5	4	7	3	9
4	3	9	7	2	8	6	5	1
1	5	7	3	6	9	8	2	4

32

1	3	5	6	9	4	8	7	2
9	8	7	2	1	5	6	4	3
6	2	4	3	8	7	5	9	1
8	9	6	7	3	1	4	2	5
3	5	1	4	2	9	7	6	8
4	7	2	8	5	6	1	3	9
7	1	9	5	4	2	3	8	6
2	4	8	1	6	3	9	5	7
5	6	3	9	7	8	2	1	4

33

6	8	1	2	7	3	9	4	5
2	9	5	6	4	1	3	7	8
3	4	7	9	5	8	6	1	2
1	2	6	7	9	4	5	8	3
9	7	8	3	1	5	4	2	6
5	3	4	8	2	6	1	9	7
4	1	2	5	6	7	8	3	9
8	5	9	4	3	2	7	6	1
7	6	3	1	8	9	2	5	4

34

3	1	8	5	7	2	9	4	6
2	7	9	6	4	1	3	5	8
6	5	4	9	3	8	1	2	7
1	9	5	7	8	3	4	6	2
8	4	2	1	6	5	7	9	3
7	6	3	4	2	9	5	8	1
9	2	6	3	5	7	8	1	4
4	3	1	8	9	6	2	7	5
5	8	7	2	1	4	6	3	9

35

8	6	5	2	4	3	9	1	7
2	4	3	9	1	7	8	6	5
9	7	1	6	8	5	4	3	2
7	2	9	3	5	1	6	8	4
3	1	6	8	2	4	5	7	9
4	5	8	7	6	9	1	2	3
6	9	2	4	3	8	7	5	1
5	3	7	1	9	6	2	4	8
1	8	4	5	7	2	3	9	6

36

7	9	8	2	1	4	3	6	5
2	1	4	5	3	6	7	8	9
5	6	3	9	7	8	1	4	2
9	8	7	1	5	2	4	3	6
6	3	1	7	4	9	5	2	8
4	2	5	8	6	3	9	7	1
1	4	2	3	8	5	6	9	7
8	7	6	4	9	1	2	5	3
3	5	9	6	2	7	8	1	4

37

5	9	2	3	6	8	1	7	4
3	8	7	9	1	4	5	6	2
4	6	1	5	2	7	8	3	9
7	2	8	6	9	3	4	5	1
6	3	9	4	5	1	7	2	8
1	4	5	7	8	2	3	9	6
9	1	4	2	7	5	6	8	3
2	7	3	8	4	6	9	1	5
8	5	6	1	3	9	2	4	7

38

2	9	4	1	5	8	6	3	7
7	3	1	4	9	6	2	8	5
5	8	6	3	7	2	1	9	4
6	4	3	5	2	7	8	1	9
1	2	9	8	4	3	5	7	6
8	5	7	6	1	9	3	4	2
3	6	2	9	8	4	7	5	1
9	1	8	7	6	5	4	2	3
4	7	5	2	3	1	9	6	8

39

8	9	3	7	1	6	2	5	4
6	4	7	5	8	2	3	9	1
1	5	2	4	3	9	6	8	7
3	8	4	2	5	7	1	6	9
2	7	6	8	9	1	5	4	3
9	1	5	6	4	3	7	2	8
7	6	9	1	2	8	4	3	5
4	2	8	3	7	5	9	1	6
5	3	1	9	6	4	8	7	2

40

7	6	2	9	1	8	5	3	4
3	9	5	7	2	4	6	8	1
4	1	8	3	5	6	2	9	7
8	4	6	1	9	5	3	7	2
9	5	3	2	4	7	8	1	6
1	2	7	8	6	3	9	4	5
2	7	9	5	8	1	4	6	3
6	8	1	4	3	2	7	5	9
5	3	4	6	7	9	1	2	8

41

4	2	5	1	8	3	9	7	6
7	1	9	6	2	5	8	3	4
8	6	3	4	9	7	2	5	1
5	4	7	8	3	2	6	1	9
9	8	2	5	6	1	7	4	3
1	3	6	9	7	4	5	8	2
6	5	4	2	1	8	3	9	7
2	7	1	3	5	9	4	6	8
3	9	8	7	4	6	1	2	5

42

6	1	8	7	9	3	5	4	2
3	7	4	5	2	8	6	9	1
2	5	9	1	6	4	3	7	8
1	6	5	3	7	2	9	8	4
8	3	7	4	1	9	2	5	6
9	4	2	8	5	6	1	3	7
7	9	3	6	8	1	4	2	5
4	8	1	2	3	5	7	6	9
5	2	6	9	4	7	8	1	3

43

5	6	2	4	1	7	8	9	3
3	4	8	2	9	5	1	6	7
7	9	1	8	6	3	2	5	4
8	7	3	9	4	1	5	2	6
2	1	4	6	5	8	7	3	9
6	5	9	3	7	2	4	8	1
4	3	5	1	2	6	9	7	8
9	2	6	7	8	4	3	1	5
1	8	7	5	3	9	6	4	2

44

1	5	2	4	6	7	9	8	3
4	6	8	3	9	2	7	1	5
9	7	3	1	8	5	4	6	2
6	4	1	2	7	8	5	3	9
3	2	9	5	1	4	8	7	6
7	8	5	6	3	9	2	4	1
8	1	4	9	2	3	6	5	7
2	3	7	8	5	6	1	9	4
5	9	6	7	4	1	3	2	8

45

1	3	6	8	7	4	2	9	5
2	4	7	6	9	5	8	1	3
8	5	9	2	1	3	6	4	7
3	2	4	1	6	8	5	7	9
6	1	5	9	4	7	3	2	8
7	9	8	3	5	2	1	6	4
4	7	1	5	8	6	9	3	2
5	6	3	4	2	9	7	8	1
9	8	2	7	3	1	4	5	6

46

6	1	7	4	3	2	9	8	5
2	3	5	9	1	8	7	6	4
8	9	4	6	7	5	1	2	3
9	2	1	5	4	6	8	3	7
7	5	6	8	9	3	4	1	2
4	8	3	7	2	1	5	9	6
1	7	8	3	6	4	2	5	9
5	6	9	2	8	7	3	4	1
3	4	2	1	5	9	6	7	8

47

5	7	9	8	6	1	3	4	2
2	1	3	7	4	9	5	6	8
4	6	8	5	2	3	7	9	1
8	9	2	1	3	5	6	7	4
7	3	6	4	8	2	9	1	5
1	5	4	9	7	6	8	2	3
9	4	7	2	5	8	1	3	6
3	2	5	6	1	7	4	8	9
6	8	1	3	9	4	2	5	7

48

4	8	6	1	9	5	2	7	3
7	9	3	2	6	8	4	5	1
2	5	1	3	7	4	9	8	6
3	2	8	6	4	7	5	1	9
9	6	4	5	8	1	7	3	2
1	7	5	9	2	3	8	6	4
5	4	2	8	3	6	1	9	7
8	3	7	4	1	9	6	2	5
6	1	9	7	5	2	3	4	8

49

7	8	3	5	9	2	1	4	6
5	2	6	4	7	1	9	8	3
9	4	1	8	6	3	2	5	7
2	6	7	9	3	8	4	1	5
4	5	9	1	2	6	3	7	8
3	1	8	7	5	4	6	9	2
8	7	2	6	4	9	5	3	1
6	9	5	3	1	7	8	2	4
1	3	4	2	8	5	7	6	9

50

1	7	9	2	3	6	5	8	4
8	3	2	7	4	5	6	9	1
4	6	5	8	1	9	3	7	2
9	5	3	4	8	1	7	2	6
2	1	8	9	6	7	4	5	3
6	4	7	5	2	3	9	1	8
3	9	6	1	7	8	2	4	5
5	2	1	6	9	4	8	3	7
7	8	4	3	5	2	1	6	9

51

8	6	2	3	5	7	1	9	4
9	4	3	8	6	1	2	5	7
1	7	5	9	4	2	8	3	6
2	3	8	6	7	5	9	4	1
4	1	9	2	8	3	6	7	5
7	5	6	4	1	9	3	2	8
3	8	7	5	9	6	4	1	2
5	9	4	1	2	8	7	6	3
6	2	1	7	3	4	5	8	9

52

2	5	6	9	1	7	4	3	8
8	7	1	4	6	3	5	9	2
9	3	4	8	2	5	1	6	7
6	4	8	1	9	2	7	5	3
7	9	2	3	5	6	8	1	4
5	1	3	7	8	4	6	2	9
1	8	7	6	3	9	2	4	5
4	2	9	5	7	1	3	8	6
3	6	5	2	4	8	9	7	1

53

6	8	1	5	9	7	2	3	4
7	4	3	2	8	6	1	5	9
5	2	9	1	3	4	7	6	8
4	7	2	9	6	3	5	8	1
3	9	8	4	5	1	6	7	2
1	5	6	7	2	8	4	9	3
8	1	4	3	7	5	9	2	6
2	3	7	6	4	9	8	1	5
9	6	5	8	1	2	3	4	7

54

9	7	6	1	2	3	4	5	8
8	4	2	6	5	9	3	7	1
5	1	3	8	7	4	6	9	2
4	5	9	7	1	2	8	3	6
6	2	1	3	9	8	5	4	7
3	8	7	4	6	5	1	2	9
1	3	8	2	4	7	9	6	5
2	9	4	5	8	6	7	1	3
7	6	5	9	3	1	2	8	4

55

6	4	7	5	9	1	8	2	3
1	9	3	2	8	6	7	5	4
5	2	8	7	4	3	1	6	9
7	3	1	9	2	5	4	8	6
4	6	9	8	3	7	2	1	5
8	5	2	6	1	4	9	3	7
2	8	5	4	6	9	3	7	1
3	7	4	1	5	8	6	9	2
9	1	6	3	7	2	5	4	8

56

6	7	4	5	2	9	3	1	8
2	1	8	7	3	4	5	9	6
9	5	3	8	6	1	4	7	2
1	2	6	3	7	5	8	4	9
5	4	9	2	1	8	6	3	7
8	3	7	4	9	6	1	2	5
7	8	1	6	4	2	9	5	3
3	9	5	1	8	7	2	6	4
4	6	2	9	5	3	7	8	1

57

8	1	6	7	2	3	9	4	5
5	7	9	6	4	1	8	2	3
3	4	2	8	5	9	1	6	7
4	8	7	5	1	2	6	3	9
6	2	3	4	9	7	5	1	8
9	5	1	3	8	6	4	7	2
1	9	4	2	7	5	3	8	6
2	6	5	1	3	8	7	9	4
7	3	8	9	6	4	2	5	1

58

7	4	9	1	8	5	3	2	6
5	2	3	6	9	7	4	1	8
6	1	8	4	2	3	9	7	5
2	9	7	8	1	6	5	3	4
8	3	4	7	5	2	1	6	9
1	5	6	9	3	4	7	8	2
9	7	5	3	6	8	2	4	1
3	6	1	2	4	9	8	5	7
4	8	2	5	7	1	6	9	3

59

9	7	2	3	6	4	5	1	8
6	5	1	8	2	7	3	9	4
4	3	8	9	1	5	2	7	6
7	1	6	2	9	3	4	8	5
3	8	4	7	5	6	9	2	1
2	9	5	1	4	8	6	3	7
8	4	3	5	7	9	1	6	2
5	2	7	6	3	1	8	4	9
1	6	9	4	8	2	7	5	3

60

5	1	2	3	9	6	8	7	4
7	9	6	8	4	2	3	1	5
3	8	4	1	7	5	9	2	6
6	7	9	5	3	1	2	4	8
1	4	8	2	6	9	5	3	7
2	3	5	4	8	7	1	6	9
9	5	7	6	2	3	4	8	1
4	6	3	9	1	8	7	5	2
8	2	1	7	5	4	6	9	3

61

8	4	3	6	5	7	2	1	9
7	1	6	9	3	2	5	8	4
9	2	5	1	8	4	6	7	3
1	6	4	7	9	8	3	5	2
2	5	9	3	6	1	7	4	8
3	7	8	4	2	5	9	6	1
5	3	2	8	4	6	1	9	7
4	9	1	5	7	3	8	2	6
6	8	7	2	1	9	4	3	5

62

4	7	1	6	2	3	8	9	5
8	6	5	1	7	9	4	2	3
3	2	9	4	5	8	1	7	6
7	9	6	3	1	5	2	8	4
5	1	4	2	8	6	7	3	9
2	8	3	7	9	4	5	6	1
9	4	8	5	3	7	6	1	2
1	5	7	9	6	2	3	4	8
6	3	2	8	4	1	9	5	7

63

4	9	2	6	7	1	5	3	8
6	5	7	3	4	8	9	2	1
3	8	1	2	5	9	6	7	4
8	7	3	1	2	5	4	6	9
5	2	6	4	9	3	1	8	7
1	4	9	8	6	7	3	5	2
9	1	8	7	3	6	2	4	5
7	6	4	5	1	2	8	9	3
2	3	5	9	8	4	7	1	6

64

3	1	7	9	8	4	2	6	5
8	9	5	2	1	6	3	7	4
6	4	2	5	7	3	1	9	8
1	8	6	7	4	9	5	2	3
5	7	3	8	6	2	9	4	1
9	2	4	3	5	1	7	8	6
4	3	9	1	2	8	6	5	7
7	6	1	4	9	5	8	3	2
2	5	8	6	3	7	4	1	9

65

6	8	9	7	3	5	2	1	4
7	2	1	8	4	6	5	3	9
3	4	5	2	1	9	7	8	6
8	5	2	3	7	4	9	6	1
4	6	3	9	5	1	8	2	7
1	9	7	6	8	2	3	4	5
5	7	6	4	2	8	1	9	3
9	1	8	5	6	3	4	7	2
2	3	4	1	9	7	6	5	8

66

2	3	6	8	5	9	7	4	1
4	9	1	2	7	6	5	8	3
7	8	5	1	3	4	2	6	9
5	2	7	9	4	3	6	1	8
9	1	4	5	6	8	3	7	2
3	6	8	7	2	1	9	5	4
1	5	9	6	8	2	4	3	7
6	4	2	3	1	7	8	9	5
8	7	3	4	9	5	1	2	6

67

6	1	2	7	9	5	8	4	3
8	3	9	4	6	1	5	7	2
5	4	7	8	3	2	1	9	6
1	6	8	9	5	4	3	2	7
9	2	5	3	8	7	4	6	1
4	7	3	2	1	6	9	8	5
3	9	1	6	2	8	7	5	4
2	8	4	5	7	3	6	1	9
7	5	6	1	4	9	2	3	8

68

6	4	1	3	7	9	2	5	8
8	2	7	4	5	6	9	1	3
9	3	5	8	2	1	4	6	7
1	8	9	6	4	5	3	7	2
7	5	3	2	9	8	1	4	6
2	6	4	1	3	7	8	9	5
3	9	2	7	6	4	5	8	1
5	1	6	9	8	2	7	3	4
4	7	8	5	1	3	6	2	9

69

1	4	6	7	5	3	2	9	8
8	9	3	2	6	4	7	1	5
2	7	5	8	1	9	3	4	6
3	8	9	4	7	2	5	6	1
7	6	2	1	9	5	4	8	3
4	5	1	6	3	8	9	7	2
9	2	4	3	8	6	1	5	7
5	1	8	9	2	7	6	3	4
6	3	7	5	4	1	8	2	9

70

8	1	9	7	4	3	2	6	5
7	6	4	5	2	1	9	3	8
3	5	2	9	8	6	1	4	7
6	3	1	4	9	5	8	7	2
2	9	8	6	1	7	3	5	4
5	4	7	2	3	8	6	1	9
1	2	6	8	5	4	7	9	3
9	7	5	3	6	2	4	8	1
4	8	3	1	7	9	5	2	6

71

8	2	5	4	6	9	3	7	1
9	7	4	1	3	2	6	8	5
1	3	6	8	7	5	2	9	4
5	1	7	6	9	8	4	2	3
2	9	8	3	1	4	7	5	6
6	4	3	5	2	7	9	1	8
7	5	1	9	4	3	8	6	2
4	6	2	7	8	1	5	3	9
3	8	9	2	5	6	1	4	7

72

1	7	5	6	2	3	9	8	4
4	8	3	9	1	7	5	6	2
6	2	9	4	8	5	1	3	7
8	3	1	5	7	2	4	9	6
2	5	4	3	6	9	7	1	8
7	9	6	1	4	8	2	5	3
3	1	7	2	9	6	8	4	5
9	6	8	7	5	4	3	2	1
5	4	2	8	3	1	6	7	9

73

7	3	6	2	5	8	1	9	4
2	1	4	7	9	6	3	8	5
9	8	5	4	3	1	6	2	7
3	4	8	6	2	9	7	5	1
6	9	2	1	7	5	4	3	8
1	5	7	3	8	4	2	6	9
4	2	9	8	1	3	5	7	6
5	6	3	9	4	7	8	1	2
8	7	1	5	6	2	9	4	3

74

1	2	6	9	4	8	3	5	7
4	7	3	2	5	6	9	1	8
9	5	8	3	1	7	2	6	4
3	6	1	8	7	4	5	9	2
7	9	5	6	2	3	8	4	1
2	8	4	1	9	5	6	7	3
8	4	9	5	3	1	7	2	6
6	1	2	7	8	9	4	3	5
5	3	7	4	6	2	1	8	9

75

3	8	1	5	9	4	6	7	2
2	9	6	8	7	3	4	1	5
5	4	7	2	6	1	9	8	3
9	3	5	1	4	6	7	2	8
7	6	8	9	2	5	3	4	1
4	1	2	7	3	8	5	6	9
1	5	9	4	8	7	2	3	6
8	7	3	6	5	2	1	9	4
6	2	4	3	1	9	8	5	7

76

1	8	7	5	3	9	6	2	4
3	9	4	6	7	2	5	1	8
2	5	6	4	1	8	3	7	9
8	3	2	9	5	7	1	4	6
5	6	1	3	8	4	7	9	2
7	4	9	2	6	1	8	5	3
4	7	8	1	2	6	9	3	5
9	1	3	8	4	5	2	6	7
6	2	5	7	9	3	4	8	1

77

8	4	2	3	1	7	6	5	9
7	1	5	2	9	6	4	8	3
6	3	9	5	8	4	2	1	7
4	9	6	1	7	2	8	3	5
5	7	3	6	4	8	1	9	2
1	2	8	9	3	5	7	4	6
9	6	1	8	2	3	5	7	4
2	8	7	4	5	9	3	6	1
3	5	4	7	6	1	9	2	8

78

4	1	9	5	6	8	7	3	2
3	6	5	2	1	7	4	9	8
7	2	8	4	3	9	6	5	1
9	3	7	8	2	1	5	4	6
8	5	2	7	4	6	3	1	9
1	4	6	9	5	3	8	2	7
2	7	4	6	9	5	1	8	3
5	8	1	3	7	2	9	6	4
6	9	3	1	8	4	2	7	5

79

4	2	8	6	3	1	5	7	9
1	3	5	9	8	7	2	6	4
9	7	6	2	5	4	3	1	8
6	9	1	5	4	8	7	2	3
7	8	4	3	2	6	9	5	1
3	5	2	1	7	9	4	8	6
8	1	3	7	9	2	6	4	5
5	4	7	8	6	3	1	9	2
2	6	9	4	1	5	8	3	7

80

2	7	4	6	3	8	9	5	1
6	3	5	1	9	7	2	4	8
8	1	9	2	4	5	7	3	6
9	4	6	8	7	1	5	2	3
7	2	8	3	5	9	1	6	4
3	5	1	4	2	6	8	9	7
1	6	2	5	8	3	4	7	9
5	8	7	9	6	4	3	1	2
4	9	3	7	1	2	6	8	5

81

9	5	6	1	8	2	3	7	4
1	8	3	7	6	4	2	5	9
2	7	4	3	9	5	8	6	1
7	6	5	9	3	8	4	1	2
4	3	9	2	1	7	6	8	5
8	2	1	4	5	6	9	3	7
5	1	8	6	4	9	7	2	3
6	4	2	5	7	3	1	9	8
3	9	7	8	2	1	5	4	6

82

1	2	7	3	9	5	4	6	8
9	3	6	8	4	2	5	7	1
4	8	5	7	1	6	9	2	3
8	1	9	5	6	4	7	3	2
6	5	2	9	7	3	8	1	4
3	7	4	2	8	1	6	9	5
7	4	1	6	3	8	2	5	9
2	9	8	1	5	7	3	4	6
5	6	3	4	2	9	1	8	7

83

9	7	8	5	6	2	1	3	4
2	4	1	7	3	9	5	6	8
3	5	6	1	4	8	9	7	2
5	6	2	4	8	3	7	9	1
7	9	3	2	1	5	8	4	6
8	1	4	6	9	7	3	2	5
1	2	5	3	7	6	4	8	9
4	8	7	9	2	1	6	5	3
6	3	9	8	5	4	2	1	7

84

6	3	5	2	7	8	9	4	1
4	9	8	1	6	3	5	7	2
2	1	7	5	9	4	3	8	6
7	5	1	8	2	9	4	6	3
3	8	2	7	4	6	1	5	9
9	6	4	3	1	5	7	2	8
1	7	9	6	5	2	8	3	4
8	4	6	9	3	7	2	1	5
5	2	3	4	8	1	6	9	7

85

7	3	9	2	6	5	1	4	8
5	8	4	1	7	3	2	6	9
2	1	6	9	8	4	7	3	5
6	7	3	5	2	9	8	1	4
8	9	1	7	4	6	3	5	2
4	2	5	3	1	8	6	9	7
3	4	2	6	9	7	5	8	1
1	5	8	4	3	2	9	7	6
9	6	7	8	5	1	4	2	3

86

4	9	1	3	2	5	7	8	6
5	7	8	6	1	9	2	3	4
3	6	2	4	7	8	9	1	5
6	8	4	1	5	7	3	9	2
7	3	5	2	9	6	8	4	1
1	2	9	8	4	3	5	6	7
2	1	7	9	8	4	6	5	3
8	5	3	7	6	1	4	2	9
9	4	6	5	3	2	1	7	8

87

5	8	2	4	3	7	9	1	6
3	9	1	6	5	8	4	7	2
7	4	6	9	2	1	8	5	3
1	5	3	7	6	9	2	8	4
8	6	7	2	4	3	1	9	5
9	2	4	1	8	5	6	3	7
4	7	8	3	9	6	5	2	1
6	1	5	8	7	2	3	4	9
2	3	9	5	1	4	7	6	8

88

7	6	4	2	8	5	9	3	1
1	8	5	6	9	3	7	4	2
9	3	2	4	1	7	6	5	8
4	1	9	5	6	8	3	2	7
2	7	6	9	3	4	8	1	5
8	5	3	1	7	2	4	9	6
6	4	8	3	5	1	2	7	9
3	9	1	7	2	6	5	8	4
5	2	7	8	4	9	1	6	3

89

3	4	8	6	1	2	9	5	7
6	7	2	5	9	3	4	8	1
5	9	1	8	4	7	3	2	6
2	1	3	7	6	9	8	4	5
9	6	4	1	5	8	2	7	3
8	5	7	2	3	4	6	1	9
1	2	5	9	8	6	7	3	4
4	8	9	3	7	1	5	6	2
7	3	6	4	2	5	1	9	8

90

6	9	2	4	8	3	1	5	7
3	7	8	1	5	6	2	9	4
1	5	4	9	7	2	6	8	3
5	6	1	7	2	4	8	3	9
2	3	7	5	9	8	4	6	1
8	4	9	3	6	1	7	2	5
9	2	3	6	4	7	5	1	8
7	8	5	2	1	9	3	4	6
4	1	6	8	3	5	9	7	2

91

9	2	3	8	4	7	6	5	1
8	5	7	1	6	3	4	2	9
1	4	6	9	2	5	8	7	3
2	9	8	4	5	1	3	6	7
6	1	5	7	3	9	2	8	4
3	7	4	6	8	2	1	9	5
4	3	9	2	7	8	5	1	6
5	8	1	3	9	6	7	4	2
7	6	2	5	1	4	9	3	8

92

7	1	5	4	2	8	9	6	3
6	8	2	9	3	7	4	1	5
3	4	9	1	5	6	7	2	8
5	2	7	8	9	1	3	4	6
9	6	8	3	4	2	5	7	1
4	3	1	7	6	5	8	9	2
8	7	4	6	1	3	2	5	9
1	5	3	2	7	9	6	8	4
2	9	6	5	8	4	1	3	7

93

4	9	7	3	8	1	2	6	5
3	1	6	4	2	5	7	9	8
8	5	2	7	6	9	4	1	3
5	6	9	2	4	3	1	8	7
1	3	4	9	7	8	6	5	2
2	7	8	1	5	6	9	3	4
7	8	5	6	9	2	3	4	1
9	2	1	8	3	4	5	7	6
6	4	3	5	1	7	8	2	9

94

6	9	7	5	2	8	3	1	4
3	8	4	7	6	1	5	9	2
5	2	1	9	3	4	8	6	7
4	3	8	1	5	7	9	2	6
2	1	9	3	8	6	4	7	5
7	6	5	2	4	9	1	8	3
9	4	2	6	1	5	7	3	8
1	5	3	8	7	2	6	4	9
8	7	6	4	9	3	2	5	1

95

8	3	7	5	6	1	2	4	9
1	4	9	3	7	2	6	5	8
2	6	5	9	8	4	1	7	3
6	5	2	8	4	3	9	1	7
4	8	3	1	9	7	5	6	2
7	9	1	6	2	5	8	3	4
3	2	6	7	5	8	4	9	1
5	7	8	4	1	9	3	2	6
9	1	4	2	3	6	7	8	5

96

3	7	4	1	2	5	6	9	8
9	1	8	7	3	6	4	5	2
5	2	6	9	8	4	3	1	7
1	4	9	2	6	7	8	3	5
2	6	5	8	4	3	1	7	9
7	8	3	5	1	9	2	4	6
4	3	7	6	5	2	9	8	1
8	5	2	4	9	1	7	6	3
6	9	1	3	7	8	5	2	4

97

6	7	2	8	3	9	4	5	1
3	5	4	6	1	7	8	9	2
1	8	9	2	5	4	3	7	6
8	9	7	4	2	1	6	3	5
5	1	3	9	8	6	2	4	7
2	4	6	5	7	3	9	1	8
9	3	5	7	6	2	1	8	4
4	6	8	1	9	5	7	2	3
7	2	1	3	4	8	5	6	9

98

4	6	2	5	9	1	8	3	7
3	5	8	2	6	7	9	1	4
7	1	9	4	8	3	2	5	6
8	2	6	1	5	4	7	9	3
1	9	3	7	2	8	4	6	5
5	7	4	9	3	6	1	2	8
6	4	7	3	1	9	5	8	2
2	3	1	8	7	5	6	4	9
9	8	5	6	4	2	3	7	1

99

8	6	3	1	5	7	2	9	4
2	7	1	9	6	4	5	3	8
5	9	4	2	3	8	7	1	6
6	8	2	4	1	9	3	5	7
3	4	9	6	7	5	1	8	2
7	1	5	8	2	3	4	6	9
1	3	8	7	4	6	9	2	5
9	5	7	3	8	2	6	4	1
4	2	6	5	9	1	8	7	3

100

5	1	7	3	8	6	4	9	2
3	9	4	1	7	2	5	8	6
8	6	2	5	9	4	1	3	7
1	8	5	9	6	3	2	7	4
9	4	6	2	1	7	8	5	3
2	7	3	8	4	5	9	6	1
4	5	1	7	3	9	6	2	8
6	3	9	4	2	8	7	1	5
7	2	8	6	5	1	3	4	9

Appreciation

This books reflects the creation of unity through diversity. Many people globally, spanning millennia, contributed to this project. Their talents and wisdom enhance the ineffable expression of the yoga of the Tao.

That awesome book cover illustration and the sacred geometry nine pointed star puzzle logo were created by Rick Smith.

Vast waves of appreciation for her exquisitely extraordinary editorial contributions flow abundantly to Melissa Morgan. From the elimination of all extraneous words to creating the semi colon bump, she has been a precious treasure in my writing process in addition to my life!

The Meta-Thoughts® by Ingrid Coffin in the Introduction are used by permission. You may subscribe to her weekly messages at www.MetaThoughts.com

All quotes by Lao-Tzu are from one the versions of the Tao Te Ching available in the public domain. There are three

Puzzle 92- Pema Chödrön quoted from James Kullander's interview with her published in The Sun Magazine, January 2005. Used by permission.

Paula Wansley, my multi-talented assistant extraordinaire, created and enhanced several images including the Puzzle Number Table.

These images were created by many talented artists globally and licensed on Dreamstime.com

Introduction- Yin Yang-© Hospitalera
Let's Play- Yin Yang Star Man- © Rolffimages; Yin and Yang-© Marincas_andrei
Sudoku, Spirituality and Surrender- Yin yang badges-© Grandeduc
What Does Math Have to do with It?- Yin Yang Heart-© Rolffimages
The Yoga of Sudoku- Yoga meditation-© Dedesuke3
The Story of Sudoku- World Turtle-© Elena Schweitzer, Ba gua scheme- © Elyomas
Magic Squares- Abstract math number background. Vector Illustration-© Kannaa; Jigsaw puzzle blank template 3x3-© Binik1; Balance concept- © Sergey Khakimullin
Step into the Mystery- Meditation and Yin Yang-© Stephanie Valentin-ranc; Ying Yang Key Means Spiritual Peace Harmony-© Stuart Miles; Binary Yin Yang-© Artaniss8
Puzzle Pointers: Progress and Play- Business Man with Yin Yang T Shirt-© Ijdema
Stay Sharp with Sudoku- Yin Yang Stones-© Alisali

Our Ever Evolving Brains- 3d Small Person yin yang-© Damirlucky

Brains Just Want to Have Fun- Skills for Right and Left Hemisphere-© T.L. Furrer; Yin Yang and human head-© Derberby

You Did It!- Yin and Yang- Ⓒ Cccsss

Endgame- Hands Holding Yin Yang Symbol-© Yuliaglam; Yin Yang Concept-© Sergey Khakimullin

Appreciation- Yin Yang on the beach-© Kasparart

Gratitude- Balance Concept © Sergey Khakimullin

Gratitude

This book has been a wonderful process from initial inspirational insight to real-live-on-the-planet-manifestation of book-in-hand. Nourishing and wrangling this vision from concept to completion allowed me the opportunity to ask for assistance from an extraordinary community of beautiful souls who were kind enough to offer opinions and guidance. I am grateful to each of you for your ongoing enthusiastic support and encouragement.

A big group hug to the Tao of Sudoku play group- Bertha Edington, Betsy Moura, Darity Wesley, Debbie Clark, Denise Lewis Premschak, Ingrid Coffin, Lana Finley,

Maryann Brown Sperry, Melissa Morgan, Paula Wansley, Richard Jelusich, Sharyn Fischer, Sherry Zak Morris, and Susannah Harte.

Heart-felt gratitude to Darity Wesley who provided her much appreciated expert legal-eyes on this project.

Special thanks to Bill for his daily kind, caring and loving presence in my life

Biographies

Cristina and Rick Smith

Cristina and Rick spent their formative years playing games for hours upon hours together. Card games, jigsaw puzzles and board games were our favorites. Our parents encouraged us to be curious, creative and communicative. They gave us the tools, like lots of trips to the library, to nurture our intellects and discover answers for ourselves. They encouraged us to be independent thinkers. Most of all, they gave us the philosophical foundation that we could do anything we wanted.

At first glance, our shared underlying basis isn't easy to see as we are quite different personalities. We have embodied those principles in diverse seeming ways, yet we could be seen as two sides of a coin. In this book, Rick is the puzzle master and book designer. Cristina is the word smith and project orchestrator.

Rick has traveled the planet extensively and Cristina has traveled the inner worlds expansively. Rick developed some of the magic of today's technology and Cristina works the magic of subtle energy healing. Rick has worked with his community of longtime friends over the years to design and produce challengingly fun games and Cristina engages her community of longtime friends to create extraordinary events.

We have lots of fun when we get together, still doing puzzles and playing games. We are delighted you decided to play with us!

For more information, visit www.SudokuWisdom.com

Made in the USA
Lexington, KY
31 October 2016